THE UNCOMMON MINISTER

Principles On The Path To A Victorious Ministry

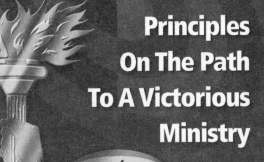

VOLUME 4

MIKE MURDOCK

TABLE OF CONTENTS

The Uncommon Minister, Volume 4
Copyright © 1999 by Mike Murdock
ISBN 1-56394-103-1

Published by The Wisdom Center
P. O. Box 99 • Denton, Texas 76202

To avoid the burdensome verbage of him/her; his, hers throughout this book, the simple reference to all of mankind, male or female, is simply "he" or "him."

≈ 1 ≈

See The Bible As The Success Handbook For Your Ministry.

The Bible is your Success Handbook.

It hit me this morning while my father and I were in prayer of what I would *not* know had the Bible not been given to me.

9 Rewards Of The Word

1. *I Would Not Recognize The Weapons God Had Given Me For All Of My Battles With Satan.* I would not know anything about the weapon of praise, the weapon of singing, the weapon of intercession. I would not know that His Word was my greatest weapon. I would not know the effects of simply *resisting* satan.

2. *I Would Not Know Anything About The Fears Of My Enemy.* I would not even be aware that satan is afraid of me. (Read Matthew 4, Luke 4, and the temptations of Christ.)

3. *I Would Not Know Anything About The Angels Assigned To Assist Me.* I would totally be ignorant of the daily ministry of angels. "But to which of the angels said He at any time, Sit on My right hand, until I make thine enemies thy footstool?

Are they not all ministering spirits, sent forth to minister for them who shall be heirs of salvation?" (Hebrews 1:13,14).

4. *I Would Be Ignorant Of The Holy Spirit Who Is Within Me And Beside Me*. I would have no knowledge at all of His power or know how to *access His presence through singing*. "Make a joyful noise unto the Lord, all ye lands. Serve the Lord with gladness: come before His presence with singing" (Psalm 100:2).

"But the Comforter, which is the Holy Ghost, Whom the Father will send in My name, He shall teach you all things, and bring all things to your remembrance, whatsoever I have said unto you" (John 14:26).

"But ye shall receive power, after that the Holy Ghost is come upon you: and ye shall be witnesses unto Me both in Jerusalem, and in all Judaea, and in Samaria, and unto the uttermost part of the earth" (Acts 1:8).

Everything worth knowing comes through the Scriptures. Everything you need to know to succeed in your ministry is in the Word of God. "Blessed is the man that feareth the Lord, that delighteth greatly in His commandments. His Seed shall be mighty upon earth: the generation of the upright shall be blessed. Wealth and riches shall be in his house: and his righteousness endureth for ever" (Psalm 112:1-4).

5. *I Would Not Know How To Judge The Behavior, The Conduct And The Words Of Other Men*. I would be deceived a thousand times more if I didn't have the Scriptures to judge other men's

conduct and their words. "As it is written, There is none righteous, no, not one: There is none that understandeth, there is none that seeketh after God. They are all gone out of the way, they are together become unprofitable; there is none that doeth good, no, not one. Their throat is an open sepulchre; with their tongues they have used deceit; the poison of asps is under their lips: Whose mouth is full of cursing and bitterness: Their feet are swift to shed blood: Destruction and misery are in their ways: And the way of peace have they not known: *There is no fear of God* before their eyes" (Romans 3:10-18).

6. *I Would Be Totally Ignorant Regarding The Reward System In The Scriptures*. The Holy Spirit promised rewards for my obedience, for the battles that I win, for each labor of love. "And whosoever shall give to drink unto one of these little ones a cup of cold water only in the name of a disciple, verily I say unto you, he shall in no wise lose his reward" (Matthew 10:42). "If ye be willing and obedient, ye shall eat the good of the land" (Isaiah 1:19).

7. *I Would Have No Knowledge Heaven Was An Ultimate Reward For Me If I Endured And Lived A Holy Life*. "In My Father's house are many mansions: if it were not so, I would have told you. I go to prepare a place for you" (John 14:2).

8. *I Would Have No Warning Of The Eternal Torment Of Hell Awaiting If I Refused To Obey The Laws Of God*. "And he cried and said, Father Abraham, have mercy on me, and send Lazarus, that he may dip the tip of his finger in water, and cool my tongue; for I am tormented in this flame" (Luke 16:24).

9. *I Would Have No Motivation In Me To Withdraw From Evil And Abandon Myself To Righteousness.* There is no pull within without the Word of God operating in me. "Thy Word have I hid in mine heart, that I might not sin against Thee" (Psalm 119:11).

Oh, think of the importance of the Word of God in your own life! No father would have any guidelines on raising his children! No mother would have standards by which to teach her children. Embrace the Holy Word of God with all your heart.

Believe it.

Listen to it on tape.

Memorize it daily.

Obey it.

Pray it aloud.

Preach it.

Study it.

See The Bible As The Success Handbook For Your Ministry.

It is One of the Secrets of the Uncommon Minister.

⚍ 2 ⚎

PREACH WHAT YOU WANT YOUR PEOPLE TO EXPERIENCE.

Whatever you preach will occur.

Billy Graham preaches salvation. What happens? Thousands make decisions to come to Christ and personally experience that salvation.

Richard Roberts preaches on The Healing Jesus. What occurs under his ministry? Thousands receive the healing touch of Jesus of Nazareth.

▶ Whatever you *teach* your people will become the *experience* of their life.
▶ What they *hear* determines what they *pursue*.
▶ What they *pursue* will determine what they *experience*.

If you refuse to minister the healing power of Jesus, disease, sickness and pain will flourish among your people.

Any Uncontested Enemy Succeeds.

Dr. Fredrick K. C. Price wrote an excellent book, "Practical Suggestions for Successful Ministry." On page 19, concerning past years he says, "The reason why no one ever received healing was because no one ever preached the Word on Divine healing."

If you refuse to teach the principles of financial

blessing to your people, debt and poverty will flourish. Anger and resentment will seethe under the surface in every home.

▶ *An Unexposed Enemy Will Master Any People.*

▶ *An Unconfronted Enemy Is An Accepted Enemy.*

It is *your* responsibility to set captives free.

You are their *Deliverer.*

You see their enemy.

You must *expose* their enemy.

You must *confront* their enemy.

Teach your people how to *overcome* that enemy.

3 Messages Every Minister Should Preach

1. *When You Preach Supernatural Love, Hatred Will Die.* Caring, compassion and love will become the qualities of the people who hear your Seeds of Wisdom on the love of God.

2. *When You Preach The Wrath Of God, The Fear Of God Will Be Birthed In Your People.* That fear of God will become the beginning of their Wisdom. Their hatred for evil will grow.

3. *When You Preach On The Return Of Christ, A Godly Hope Will Rise In The Hearts Of Every Family.* The signs of the time will become more meaningful to them. "And every man that hath this hope in Him purifieth himself, even as He is pure" (1 John 3:3).

None of us knows everything.

Remember Every Minister Is Ignorant In Some Area. That's why God created so many of us. The body of Christ can be ministered to effectively through the variation of callings and anointings. It's common among doctors. The ear doctor may be next door to a throat doctor. The pianist is not necessarily effective on the drums. Both are musicians, with different gifts.

Follow The Example Of Successful Pastors Who Schedule Other Ministries Whose Focus Differs From Their Own. One minister friend of mine feels inadequate to teach on financial prosperity. He calls in other teaching ministries who present the message effectively to his people. Another pastor friend of mine said, "I simply do not understand how Bible prophecy links up with today's events. My church responsibilities at the hospitals, counseling and overseeing the business transactions have robbed me of the time needed to develop my Wisdom in the area of Bible prophecy. But, twice a year I bring other ministries in for one week to teach every night and day that message and part of the gospel to my people."

This is Wisdom.

Whatever You Lack Is Hidden In Someone Else Near You. Drop your pail in their well!

Value The Focus Of Other Ministries Around You. You see, the man who preaches soul winning may lack Wisdom on the Return of Christ. His focus is soul winning. Treasure his calling. Another minister, whose focus is prayer and fasting, may not understand the Laws of Financial Prosperity. But, he loves the presence of God and moves freely and comfortably in the areas of receiving answers to prayer. Honor his focus.

Preach What You Want Your People To Experience.

It is One of the Secrets of The Uncommon Minister.

≈ 3 ≈

KNOW YOUR SHEEP.

Your sheep are worth knowing.

Jesus commanded Peter, "Feed My sheep" (John 21:16). This verse is pregnant with Wisdom.

Jesus *loved* people.

Jesus *sought out* the lonely, *encouraged* the downcast and *corrected* the wayward.

Jesus wanted His disciples to value, cherish and treasure the opportunity to love the lost and feed His sheep.

6 Things Every Minister Should Know About The Sheep

1. *Know Their Assignment.* Your people have incredible qualities. Patience? Kindness? Some are going through the most difficult trials of their life. Yet, they keep a sweet spirit.

As you look across the audience, you're looking into the face of overcomers, fighters and victors.

How *important* are they to you?

Are they simply *numbers*?

Do you ever call their names before the Lord?

Are you aware of their *Assignment*?

2. *Know Their Dominant Gifts, Skills And Strengths.* The Holy Spirit planted uncommon talents within them. Do you know what those gifts really are? Do you know what each person in your

congregation does *daily*? Certainly, when your church is a huge one attended by thousands, that is impossible to some degree. But your *concern* should exist. Your caring should be *obvious*.

3. *Know Their Background*. You see, the pain we experienced in our childhood often affects the *decisions* we make, the *offenses* we collect and the *fears* that are birthed.

Never Preach To The Needs You Do Not Feel.

4. *Know Their Weaknesses*. Jesus said, "Simon, behold, Satan hath desired to have you, that he may sift you as wheat: But I have prayed for thee," (Luke 22:31,32).

Peter heard this.

Peter felt loved.

Peter knew Jesus interceded for him daily.

How can you pray *effectively* for those whose weaknesses you have not yet discovered?

5. *Know Their Passion And Obsession*. You see, your people will invest time, energy and finances into their obsession and passion. Jesus did this. He showed up on the shores of Galilee. He even interrogated His disciples, "Have ye any meat?" He wanted to know about their fishing success. True interest is so rare.

Genuine concern is the greatest gift you can give. It always begins a miracle relationship.

6. *Know Their Struggles*. You are busy, as a minister of the gospel, supervising many projects, staff members and situations. But your people are hurting. That young couple in the back of the sanctuary may be battling to pay the rent on their apartment.

The single mother is struggling against anger

and hate because her ex-husband refuses to provide her any child support.

The teenagers on the back row feel unwanted and unloved. They are struggling for a sense of significance and worth.

Do *you* remember that?

Do you *feel* that?

Are you *changing that*?

The words of Jesus ring clear, "My sheep hear My voice, and I know them, and they follow Me" (John 10:27). Why? He had invested time and attention in the relationship. "Know them that labor among you." (See 1 Timothy 5:12).

4 Powerful Ways To Increase Your Knowledge Of Your People

1.   Have Your People Fill Out Questionnaires, Send You Pictures Of Their Business And Describe Their Greatest Needs.

2.   Keep A Prayer Book In Your Secret Place With The Photographs And Desires Of Your People And Their Families.

3.   Train Qualified Spiritual Leaders For Different Groups In Your Church Who Will *Know* Them.

4.   Schedule A Variety Of Meetings, Events And Celebrations. Some have special concerts for youth, birthday parties, and graduation celebrations. Why? Just to *know* your people.

Jesus knows you. That is the reason for your loyalty to Him.

Know Your Sheep.

It is One of the Secrets of The Uncommon Minister.

☙ 4 ❧

NEVER MAKE IMPORTANT MINISTRY DECISIONS WHEN YOU ARE TIRED.

Tired eyes rarely see a great future.
When you are weary, you change.
You don't have the kind of faith, the same kind of enthusiasm or the same kind of patience.
When you are rested, you are strengthened.

8 Undesirable Results Produced By Fatigue

1.   *When You Are Tired, Mountains Look Bigger.* When you are tired at night, things that normally would appear simple suddenly seem burdensome and very complex to you. Tasks that really require a minimal effort suddenly seem too much to take on.

2.   *When You Are Tired, Valleys Seem Deeper.* Discouraging factors seem to enlarge. Disappointment seems keener and stronger when your body is fatigued.

3.   *When You Are Tired, Offenses Come Easier.* It has happened in my own life. I seem more offended than I normally would be. *Little* things become big in my mind.

When I am tired, I often replay in my mind wrongs that people have done to me.

When I am rested, my mind moves to positive, wonderful and glorious dreams, things I want to accomplish and do.

Fatigue affects me in the opposite manner. I begin to meditate on my own mistakes and the mistakes of others. There's a Scripture that indicates that satan wants to wear out the saints. I believe it. "And he shall speak great words against the most High, and *shall wear out the saints* of the most High, and think to change times and laws: and they shall be given into his hand until a time and times and the dividing of time" (Daniel 7:25).

Jesus understood this. That's why He encouraged His disciples to "come ye apart and rest awhile." Or, as Vance Havner suggested, "Ye will come apart!" (Read Mark 6:31.)

One of the great presidents of the United States once said that he would never make a decision past 3:00 in the afternoon. His mind was too tired and weary to consider every option available.

4. *When You Are Tired, You Become Less Tolerant Of The Views Of Others.* When others are weary, they seem less understanding of your own opinions and views, too

5. *When You Are Tired, Your Focus Turns To What You Want Instead Of The Appropriate Method For Achieving It.*

6. *When You Are Tired, Your Focus Will Usually Turn To A Short-Term Goal Rather Than Your Long-Term Goals.*

7. *When You Are Tired, Your Words Will Become Rash, Inappropriate And Even Harsh Towards Those*

Who Truly Love You.

8. *When You Are Tired, You Become Unwilling To Invest The Appropriate And Sufficient Time In Planning Ahead On Projects.*

Rest restores you.

Rest energizes you.

Rest improves the quality of decision-making.

Never Make Important Ministry Decisions When You Are Tired.

It is One of the Secrets of The Uncommon Minister.

≈ 5 ≈

RESPECT THE SCHEDULE, FOCUS, AND NEEDS OF YOUR PEOPLE.

Respect the responsibilities of your people.

I had finished a two-day school of the Holy Spirit up north. It had been a glorious two days. The presence of God was so powerful. I loved being with my friends and partners, as always.

Due to the airline schedule, I had to leave 30 minutes earlier than planned. Another minister was going to conclude the session for me. Because of the airline schedule, two flights were necessary and would let me arrive at my destination at 1:00 a.m.

My schedule was tight. In fact, I would barely arrive on time at the church where I was scheduled. So, I announced to everyone present that my plane schedule was too close for me to stay afterwards for additional conversation.

Yet, as I was rushing toward the door with my briefcase, my associate by my side, five to seven people stopped me. Standing in front of me, they *insisted* that I autograph my books they had purchased. Some insisted that I hear about an experience they had had.

Each one of them had *totally ignored my schedule,* my words, and showed little caring whatsoever.

Did they love me? Not really.

They loved *themselves*.

Their only obsession was *to get something* they wanted, regardless of the toll it took on me.

My needs meant little to them. My schedule was unimportant to them.

The Holy Spirit is always offended by such insensitivity and lack of caring for others.

Always Make Sure Your Time With Someone Is Appropriate For Their Schedule. Do not use intimidating language or statements. One that I often hear is, "Do you have any time for *me*." This simply an attempt to intimidate me. Or, statements like, "You *never* have time for me. You *always* have time for *everyone else!*"

This is *victim* vocabulary. This kind of person has no true regard for others. They are obsessed with themselves. You can never give them enough time and attention to satisfy them.

Always mark those who show disregard and disrespect for your time, the most precious gift God gave you. One pastor here in Dallas refuses any personal counseling to newcomers. They must qualify for private counseling by attending six continuous weeks of his teaching services. Those Who Abuse Your Time Will Misuse Your Wisdom.

Honor the work schedule and unique family needs of your people. As an evangelist, it has taken years to understand this key. Since I come to a church only once a year, I always expect everyone to drop everything they are doing to attend my special conference! Sometimes, people have to rush out because of their jobs and other responsibilities.

One night, I was startled to see a man leave as I was speaking. In my brashness, I publicly questioned him rather jokingly.

"Are you angry at my ministry?" I asked.

He looked back so embarrassed as everyone stared at him.

"I'm late for my work shift tonight," he replied quietly.

Embarrassed, I could have crawled under the front seat. I simply had not understood *his* schedule.

Successful ministers recognize that many mothers have restless children; many fathers work long hours. They honor and respect this, and their people appreciate this respect.

Respect The Schedule, Focus And Needs Of Your People.

It is One of the Secrets of The Uncommon Minister.

≈ 6 ≈

AVOID THE TRAP OF UNANSWERABLE QUESTIONS.

Satan asked the first question.

Accept the fact: you are not God. That's why the Apostle Paul wrote to his protégé, "But foolish and underlearned questions avoid, knowing that they do gender strifes" (2 Timothy 2:23).

I have a tenacious curiosity. My mind is in constant pursuit of answers and solutions. There is nothing really wrong with desiring truthful answers. Everyone knows that.

However, it was a *simple question* in the beautiful and gorgeous Garden of Eden *that birthed the greatest tragedy* that has ever occurred in the history of man.

Satan asked the first question on record. "Now the serpent was more subtle than any beast of the field which the Lord God had made. And he said unto the woman, yea, hath God said, Ye shall not eat of every tree in the garden?" (Genesis 3:1).

He set the trap.

Doubt was the bait.

Eve fell for it.

Adam followed.

You and I have paid a dear price for this tragic mistake.

Ask the questions God likes to answer.

The obedient ask, "*What* must I do?"

The disobedient ask, "*Why* should I do it?"

Discern questions nobody is qualified to answer. I remember sitting around a table asking stupid questions such as, "Which came first, the chicken or the egg?" In my early ministry, I remember sitting on a Greyhound bus trying to answer a question from a cynical old man, "Who did Cain marry?" What a waste of time!

Laugh at the attempts of cynics to intimidate you with difficult questions. Don't get angry. You see, the cynic is not living the answers he *already* knows in his heart. He is using questions *as a smoke screen* to distract you from his own rebellion. The Pharisees tried this. Jesus moved *away* from them and went home with Zacchaeus who recognized his need of Jesus.

Stop trying to answer unanswerable questions about divine healing. One of the greatest and most effective men in our generation is Oral Roberts. He once said, "I can't figure out healing. I pray for some I don't think will be healed, and God heals them. I pray for others I just know will be healed, and they don't receive it. *It's all still a mystery to me.*" He doesn't play God.

Don't try to explain tragedies. Nobody can fully explain why someone is healed and another dies. My own parents cannot explain the death of two of their children. But, they have embraced the goodness of God and the "evilness" of satan. God gives life, and satan takes life. (Read John 10:10.) Thousands leave the Highway of Answers to build their entire conversation around the Pothole of Questions.

You can't climb mountains studying pebbles.

Often, after delivering powerful Wisdom Keys on Success, I have been approached by someone who ignored everything I taught that night. They had searched for one possible question that would "stump me." In my beginning years, I thought they were sincere. I wasted hundreds of hours trying to become "The Answer Man" to everybody. It was ridiculous!

What To Do When Someone Asks You An Unanswerable Question

1. Invite Them To Pray With You For The Spirit Of Wisdom To Reveal Answers.

2. Recommend An Appropriate Book Or Specific Scriptures That Are Helpful.

3. Invite Them To Invest In A Tape Of Your Ministry That Could Revolutionize Their Life.

Their response to your three suggestions reveals the depth of their true appetite for wisdom.

Time wasters are everywhere. I meet them daily. Time is the most precious gift I have, and I refuse to permit a cynic or a fool to destroy it.

Avoid The Trap Of Unanswerable Questions.

It is One of the Secrets of the Uncommon Minister.

❧ 7 ❧

STOP HURRYING YOUR OFFERINGS.

Good things take time.

The mentorship of Jesus required 30 years. The training of Moses required 80 years. "The Lord is good unto them that wait for Him" (Lamentations 3:25).

I am appalled at the disrespect shown toward Offerings.

The Holy Spirit is grieved over the disrespect shown toward Offerings.

▶ The Offering Is A Love Moment With God.
▶ The Offering Is The Golden Door To Harvest.
▶ The Offering Is The Season For Thanksgiving And Worship.

The Uncommon Minister knows this and gives quality time to the celebration of the tithes and offerings to our heavenly Father, the Uncommon Provider.

Fewer than 20 times in my life have I attended any service where I have had sufficient time to secure my checkbook and write a check before the usher appeared by my side.

It takes time for the focus of people to change from watching an interesting choir to understanding the value of their Seed. Your church members have lived in a climate of doubt for seven days, 168 hours of fear and unbelief. The television news has made them scared and fearful of the volatile changes facing the banks. Unexpected bills have arrived in the mail. The roof suddenly leaks. The car breaks down. An expected promotion becomes a disappointment. Now, your church member sits there on Sunday morning with his head whirling with thoughts and questions such as, "How will I squeeze a new alternator into my budget? Where will I get the money to put my son through college? How will we get the second car that we desperately need?"

Suddenly, the minister appears and makes a statement in the midst of this volcanic eruption of doubts and financial fears and says, "Will the ushers come forward as we receive the morning tithes and offerings?"

Disengaging from these thoughts of debt, credit cards and impending bills...is a miracle within itself.

Your people deserve quality time to hear from your burning heart what you know about their promised Harvest. They are facing a mountain of bills. Their mind is in torment because their mate made an unexpected and unwise purchase. Their car repair bill was horrendous. And you are suddenly rushing them to bring their tithe and offerings to God?

Talk to them.

Talk to their *heart*.

Address their *hopes*.

Remove their doubts.

The Word of God *will* work for them.

Focus their attention on the Lord of the Harvest, the God who will *not* fail them.

Impregnate their Seeds with a vision...a Portrait of the Promise of Uncommon Provision. Elijah did when he approached the widow of Zarephath. (See 1 Kings 17.) Paint an accurate picture of Hope for them.

That's what The Offering is about.

The Offering is not to pay for the new roof of the sanctuary, to buy an extra ten acres of ground next door, or to pay your salary.

The Seeds of your people are pregnant with their future.

Make the moment *count*.

Make it a *great* moment.

Make it a *hopeful* moment.

Make it a *mentorship* moment.

Make it a *love* moment.

Make it a *faith* moment.

Make it a *miracle* moment.

Those who really love food don't want to be rushed through this moment of pleasure in their day.

Those who enjoy loving their mate consider it an investment worthy of complete attention.

Don't rush through the most important moment of every service...the Moment of Thanksgiving, Respect and Honoring of our Uncommon Provider... our Jehovah-Jireh.

The Uncommon Minister refuses to rush through The Offering that will forever change the future of his people, his vision and his ministry.

Stop Hurrying Your Offerings.

It is One of the Secrets of The Uncommon Minister.

ABOUT MIKE MURDOCK

■ Has embraced his Assignment to pursue... possess..and publish the Wisdom of God to heal the broken in his generation.

■ Began full-time evangelism at the age of 19, which has continued for 33 years.

■ Has traveled and spoken to more than 15,000 audiences in 38 countries, including East Africa, the Orient and Europe.

■ Noted author of 115 books, including best sellers, "Wisdom for Winning", "Dream Seeds" and "The Double Diamond Principle".

■ Created the popular "Wisdom Topical Bible" series for Businessmen, Mothers, Fathers, Teenagers and the One-Minute Pocket Bible.

■ Has composed more than 5,400 songs such as "I Am Blessed", "You Can Make It", "Holy Spirit This Is Your House" and "Jesus Just The Mention Of Your Name", recorded by many artists.

■ Is the Founder of The Wisdom Center, for the training of those entering the ministry.

■ Has a weekly television program called "Wisdom Keys With Mike Murdock" and a daily radio broadcast, "The Secret Place."

■ Has appeared often on TBN, CBN and other television network programs.

■ Is a Founding Trustee on the Board of Charismatic Bible Ministries.

■ Has had more than 3,400 accept the call into full-time ministry under his ministry.

Complete your personal library of
"The Uncommon Minister" Series. These first seven
volumes are a must for your ministry reading.
Practical and powerful, these Wisdom Keys will
enhance your ministry expression for years to come.

ITEM	TITLE	QTY	PRICE	TOTAL
B107	The Uncommon Minister, Volume 1		$5.00	$
B108	The Uncommon Minister, Volume 2		$5.00	$
B109	The Uncommon Minister, Volume 3		$5.00	$
B110	The Uncommon Minister, Volume 4		$5.00	$
B111	The Uncommon Minister, Volume 5		$5.00	$
B112	The Uncommon Minister, Volume 6		$5.00	$
B113	The Uncommon Minister, Volume 7		$5.00	$
All 7 Volumes of The Uncommon Minister			$35.00	$

Mail To: **The Wisdom Center** P.O. Box 99 Denton, TX 76202 940-891-1400	Add 10% For Shipping	$
	(Canada add 20% to retail cost and 20% shipping)	$
	Enclosed Is My Seed-Faith Gift For Your Ministry	$
	Total Amount Enclosed	$

SORRY NO C.O.D.'S

Name ————————————————————————
Address ————————————————————————
City ————————————————————————
State ————————————————————————
Zip ——————————— Telephone ———————————

☐ Check ☐ Money Order
☐ Visa ☐ Master Card ☐ Amex
Signature ————————————————
Exp. Date ————————————
Card No. ————————————

———— **Quantity Prices for** ————
"The Uncommon Minister" Series

1-9	=	$5.00 each
10-99	=	$4.00 each (20% discount)
100-499	=	$3.50 each (30% discount)
500-999	=	$3.00 each (40% discount)
1,000-up	=	$2.50 each (50% discount)
5,000-up	=	$2.00 each (60% discount)

POWERFUL WISDOM BOOKS FROM DR. MIKE MURDOCK!

You can increase your Wisdom Library by purchasing any one of these great titles by *MIKE MURDOCK*. Scriptural, practical, readable. These books are life-changing!

The Covenant Of 58 Blessings

Dr. Murdock shares the phenomenon of the 58 Blessings, his experiences, testimonials, and the words of God Himself concerning the 58 Blessings. Your life will never be the same! (Paperback)
(B47) 86 pages $8

The Proverbs 31 Woman

God's ultimate woman is described in Proverbs 31. *Dr. Murdock* breaks it down to the pure revelation of these 31 marvelous qualities. (Paperback)
(B49) 68 pages $7

Wisdom - God's Golden Key To Success

In this book, *Dr. Mike Murdock* shares his insight into the Wisdom of God that will remove the veil of ignorance and propel you into the abundant life. (Paperback)
(B70) 67 pages $7

Secrets Of The Richest Man Who Ever Lived

This teaching on the life of Solomon will bring you to a higher level of understanding in the 31 secrets of uncommon wealth and success. God's best will soon be yours as you learn and put into practice these keys. (Paperback)
(B99) 192 pages $10

Remember...God sent His Son, but He left His Book!

Wisdom For Crisis Times

Discover the Wisdom Keys to dealing with tragedies, stress and times of crisis. Secrets that will unlock the answers in the right way to react in life situations. (Paperback)
(B40) 118 pages $9

The Double Diamond Principle

This explosive book contains 58 Master Secrets for Total Success in the life of Jesus that will help you achieve your goals and dreams. (Paperback)
(B39) 144 pages $9

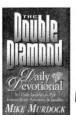

The Double Diamond Daily Devotional

This devotional for every day of the year is filled with dynamic Wisdom keys and Scriptures for successful leaders and achievers. This volume includes topics on dreams and goals, relationships, miracles, prosperity and more!
(Paperback)
(B80) 374 pages $12

Wisdom For Winning

The best-selling handbook for achieving success. Every obstacle and pitfall to abundant success is covered in this powerful volume. This book will put you in the "Winner's World." If you desire to be successful and happy, this is the book for you! (Paperback)
(B01) 220 pages $10

Thirty-One Secrets Of An Unforgettable Woman

Dynamic Wisdom Keys to unveil secrets of one of the greatest Biblical women in history, Ruth. This book will change you! (Paperback)
(B57) Over 130 pages $9

Dream Seeds

What do you dream of doing with your life? What would you attempt to do if you knew it was impossible to fail? This 118 page book helps you answer these questions and much more! (Paperback)
(B11) 118 pages $9

ORDER FORM THE MIKE MURDOCK WISDOM LIBRARY

(All books paperback unless indicated otherwise.)

QTY	CODE	BOOK TITLE	USA	TOTAL
	B01	WISDOM FOR WINNING	$10	
	B02	5 STEPS OUT OF DEPRESSION	$ 2	
	B03	THE SEX TRAP	$ 2	
	B04	10 LIES PEOPLE BELIEVE ABOUT MONEY	$ 2	
	B05	FINDING YOUR PURPOSE IN LIFE	$ 2	
	B06	CREATING TOMORROW THROUGH SEED-FAITH	$ 2	
	B07	BATTLE TECHNIQUES FOR WAR WEARY SAINTS	$ 2	
	B08	ENJOYING THE WINNING LIFE	$ 2	
	B09	FOUR FORCES/GUARANTEE CAREER SUCCESS	$ 2	
	B10	THE BRIDGE CALLED DIVORCE	$ 2	
	B11	DREAM SEEDS	$ 9	
	B12	YOUNG MINISTERS HANDBOOK	$20	
	B13	SEEDS OF WISDOM ON DREAMS AND GOALS	$ 3	
	B14	SEEDS OF WISDOM ON RELATIONSHIPS	$ 3	
	B15	SEEDS OF WISDOM ON MIRACLES	$ 3	
	B16	SEEDS OF WISDOM ON SEED-FAITH	$ 3	
	B17	SEEDS OF WISDOM ON OVERCOMING	$ 3	
	B18	SEEDS OF WISDOM ON HABITS	$ 3	
	B19	SEEDS OF WISDOM ON WARFARE	$ 3	
	B20	SEEDS OF WISDOM ON OBEDIENCE	$ 3	
	B21	SEEDS OF WISDOM ON ADVERSITY	$ 3	
	B22	SEEDS OF WISDOM ON PROSPERITY	$ 3	
	B23	SEEDS OF WISDOM ON PRAYER	$ 3	
	B24	SEEDS OF WISDOM ON FAITH TALK	$ 3	
	B25	SEEDS OF WISDOM ONE YEAR DEVOTIONAL	$10	
	B26	THE GOD BOOK	$10	
	B27	THE JESUS BOOK	$10	
	B28	THE BLESSING BIBLE	$10	
	B29	THE SURVIVAL BIBLE	$10	
	B30	TEENAGERS TOPICAL BIBLE	$ 6	
	B30L	TEENAGERS TOPICAL BIBLE (LEATHER)	$20	
	B31	ONE-MINUTE TOPICAL BIBLE	$12	
	B32	MINISTER'S TOPICAL BIBLE	$ 6	
	B33	BUSINESSMAN'S TOPICAL BIBLE	$ 6	
	B33L	BUSINESSMAN'S TOPICAL BIBLE (LEATHER)	$20	
	B34L	GRANDPARENT'S TOPICAL BIBLE (LEATHER)	$20	
	B35	FATHER'S TOPICAL BIBLE	$ 6	
	B35L	FATHER'S TOPICAL BIBLE (LEATHER)	$20	
	B36	MOTHER'S TOPICAL BIBLE	$ 6	
	B36L	MOTHER'S TOPICAL BIBLE (LEATHER)	$20	
	B37	NEW CONVERT'S BIBLE	$ 6	
	B38	THE WIDOW'S TOPICAL BIBLE	$ 6	
	B39	THE DOUBLE DIAMOND PRINCIPLE	$ 9	
	B40	WISDOM FOR CRISIS TIMES	$ 9	
	B41	THE GIFT OF WISDOM (VOLUME ONE)	$ 8	
	B42	ONE-MINUTE BUSINESSMAN'S DEVOTIONAL	$10	
	B43	ONE-MINUTE BUSINESSWOMAN'S DEVOTIONAL	$10	
	B44	31 SECRETS FOR CAREER SUCCESS	$10	
	B45	101 WISDOM KEYS	$ 7	
	B46	31 FACTS ABOUT WISDOM	$ 7	
	B47	THE COVENANT OF 58 BLESSINGS	$ 8	
	B48	31 KEYS TO A NEW BEGINNING	$ 7	
	B49	31 SECRETS OF THE PROVERBS 31 WOMAN	$ 7	
	B50	ONE-MINUTE POCKET BIBLE FOR ACHIEVERS	$ 5	
	B51	ONE-MINUTE POCKET BIBLE FOR FATHERS	$ 5	
	B52	ONE-MINUTE POCKET BIBLE FOR MOTHERS	$ 5	

Mail to: Dr. Mike Murdock • The Wisdom Training Center • P.O. Box 99 • Denton, TX 76202
(940) 891-1400 Or USA Call Toll Free **1-888-WISDOM-1**

QTY	CODE	BOOK TITLE	USA	TOTAL
	B53	ONE-MINUTE POCKET BIBLE FOR TEENAGERS	$ 5	
	B54	ONE-MINUTE DAILY DEVOTIONAL(HARDBACK)	$14	
	B55	20 KEYS TO A HAPPIER MARRIAGE	$ 2	
	B56	HOW TO TURN MISTAKES TO MIRACLES	$ 2	
	B57	31 SECRETS OF THE UNFORGETTABLE WOMAN	$ 9	
	B58	MENTOR'S MANNA ON ATTITUDE	$ 2	
	B59	THE MAKING OF A CHAMPION	$ 6	
	B60	ONE-MINUTE POCKET BIBLE FOR MEN	$ 5	
	B61	ONE-MINUTE POCKET BIBLE FOR WOMEN	$ 5	
	B62	ONE-MINUTE POCKET BIBLE FOR BUS. PROFESSIONALS	$ 5	
	B63	ONE-MINUTE POCKET BIBLE FOR TRUCKERS	$ 5	
	B64	MENTOR'S MANNA ON ACHIEVEMENT	$ 2	
	B65	MENTOR'S MANNA ON ADVERSITY	$ 2	
	B66	GREED, GOLD AND GIVING	$ 2	
	B67	GIFT OF WISDOM FOR CHAMPIONS	$ 8	
	B68	GIFT OF WISDOM FOR ACHIEVERS	$ 8	
	B69	MENTOR'S MANNA ON THE SECRET PLACE	$ 2	
	B70	GIFT OF WISDOM FOR MOTHERS	$ 8	
	B71	WISDOM-GOD'S GOLDEN KEY TO SUCCESS	$ 7	
	B72	THE DOUBLE DIAMOND DAILY DEVOTIONAL	$12	
	B73	MENTOR'S MANNA ON ABILITIES	$ 2	
	B74	THE ASSIGNMENT: DREAM/DESTINY #1	$10	
	B75	THE ASSIGNMENT: ANOINTING/ADVERSITY #2	$10	
	B76	THE ASSIGNMENT: TRIALS/TRIUMPHS #3	$10	
	B77	THE ASSIGNMENT: PAIN/PASSION #4	$10	
	B78	WISDOM KEYS FOR A POWERFUL PRAYER LIFE	$ 2	
	B79	7 OBSTACLES TO ABUNDANT SUCCESS	$ 2	
	B80	THE GREATEST SUCCESS HABIT ON EARTH	$ 2	
	B81	BORN TO TASTE THE GRAPES	$ 2	
	B82	31 REASONS PEOPLE DO NOT RECEIVE THEIR FINANCIAL HARVEST	$12	
	B83	GIFT OF WISDOM FOR WIVES	$ 8	
	B84	GIFT OF WISDOM FOR HUSBANDS	$ 8	
	B85	GIFT OF WISDOM FOR TEENAGERS	$ 8	
	B86	GIFT OF WISDOM FOR LEADERS	$ 8	
	B87	GIFT OF WISDOM FOR GRADUATES	$ 8	
	B88	GIFT OF WISDOM FOR BRIDES	$ 8	
	B89	GIFT OF WISDOM FOR GROOMS	$ 8	
	B90	GIFT OF WISDOM FOR MINISTERS	$ 8	
	B91	THE LEADERSHIP SECRETS OF JESUS(HDBK)	$15	
	B92	SECRETS OF THE JOURNEY (VOL. 1)	$ 5	
	B93	SECRETS OF THE JOURNEY (VOL. 2)	$ 5	
	B94	SECRETS OF THE JOURNEY (VOL. 3)	$ 5	
	B95	SECRETS OF THE JOURNEY (VOL. 4)	$ 5	

☐ CASH ☐ CHECK ☐ MONEY ORDER

☐ VISA ☐ MASTER CARD ☐ AMEX

CREDIT CARD #

| | | | | | | | | | | | | | | | | | | | | |

EXPIRATION DATE | | | | | *SORRY NO C.O.D.'s*

SIGNATURE _____

TOTAL PAGE 2	$
TOTAL PAGE 1	$
*ADD SHIPPING 10% USA / 20% OTHERS	$
CANADA CURRENCY DIFFERENCE ADD 20%	$
TOTAL ENCLOSED	$

PLEASE PRINT

Name _____

Address _____

City _____

State _____ Zip _____

Phone ( ) _____

WISDOM 12 PAK

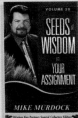

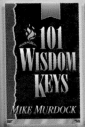

THE MASTER SECRET OF LIFE IS WISDOM
Ignorance Is The Only True Enemy Capable Of Destroying You (Hosea 4:6, Proverbs 11:14)

▶ 1.	MY PERSONAL DREAM BOOK	B143	$5.00
▶ 2.	THE COVENANT OF FIFTY EIGHT BLESSINGS	B47	$8.00
▶ 3.	WISDOM, GOD'S GOLDEN KEY TO SUCCESS	B71	$7.00
▶ 4.	SEEDS OF WISDOM ON THE HOLY SPIRIT	B116	$5.00
▶ 5.	SEEDS OF WISDOM ON THE SECRET PLACE	B115	$5.00
▶ 6.	SEEDS OF WISDOM ON THE WORD OF GOD	B117	$5.00
▶ 7.	SEEDS OF WISDOM ON THE ASSIGNMENT	B122	$5.00
▶ 8.	SEEDS OF WISDOM ON PROBLEM SOLVING	B118	$5.00
▶ 9.	101 WISDOM KEYS	B45	$7.00
▶ 10.	31 KEYS TO A NEW BEGINNING	B48	$7.00
▶ 11.	THE PROVERBS 31 WOMAN	B49	$7.00
▶ 12.	31 FACTS ABOUT WISDOM	B46	$7.00

Wisdom Is The Principal Thing
Book Pak
WBL-12 / **$30**
(A $73 Value!)
The Wisdom Center

ORDER TODAY!
www.thewisdomcenter.cc

1-888-WISDOM-1
(1-888-947-3661)

THE WISDOM CENTER • P.O. Box 99 • Denton, Texas 76202

Money Matters.

This Powerful Video will unleash the Financial Harvest of your lifetime!

- ▶ **8 Scriptural Reasons You Should Pursue Financial Prosperity**

- ▶ **The Secret Prayer Key You Need When Making A Financial Request To God**

- ▶ **The Weapon Of Expectation And The 5 Miracles It Unlocks**

- ▶ **How To Discern Those Who Qualify To Receive Your Financial Assistance**

- ▶ **How To Predict The Miracle Moment God Will Schedule Your Financial Breakthrough**

Somebody's Future
Will Not Begin Until You Enter.

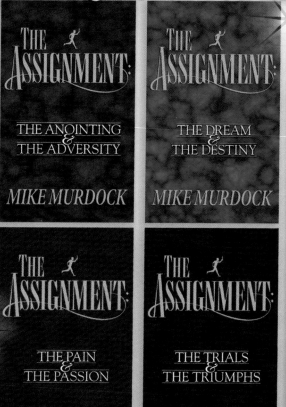

THE ASSIGNMENT:
THE ANOINTING & THE ADVERSITY
MIKE MURDOCK

THE ASSIGNMENT:
THE DREAM & THE DESTINY
MIKE MURDOCK

THE ASSIGNMENT:
THE PAIN & THE PASSION
MIKE MURDOCK

THE ASSIGNMENT:
THE TRIALS & THE TRIUMPHS
MIKE MURDOCK

THIS COLLECTION INCLUDES 4 DIFFERENT BOOKS CONTAINING UNCOMMON WISDOM FOR DISCOVERING YOUR LIFE ASSIGNMENT

▸ How To Achieve A God-Given Dream And Goal

▸ How To Know Who Is Assigned To You

▸ The Purpose And Rewards Of An Enemy

The Secret Place
Library Pak

Songs from the Secret Place

Over 40 Great Songs On 6 Music Tapes
Including "I'm In Love" / Love Songs From The Holy Spirit
Birthed In The Secret Place / <u>Side A</u> Is Dr. Mike Murdock
Singing / <u>Side B</u> Is Music Only For Your Personal Prayer Time

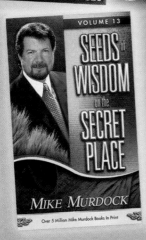

Seeds of Wisdom on the Secret Place

4 Secrets The Holy Spirit Reveals In The Secret Place / The Necessary
Ingredients In Creating Your Secret Place / 10 Miracles That Will
Happen In The Secret Place

Seeds of Wisdom on the Holy Spirit

The Protocol For Entering The Presence Of
The Holy Spirit / the greatest day of my life and
What Made It So / Power Keys For Developing Your
Personal Relationship With The Holy Spirit

Wisdom Is The Principal Thing
Book/Tape Pak
SP PAK-001 / **$30**
Six Audio Tapes & Two Books
(A $40 Value!)
The Wisdom Center

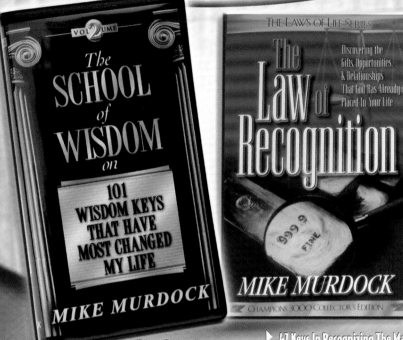

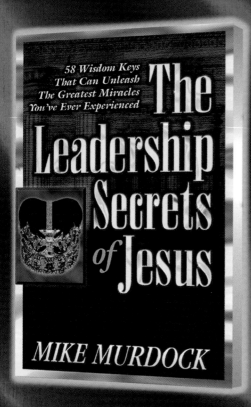

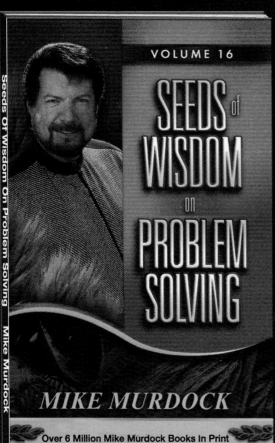

You Can Have It.

▶ Why Sickness Is Not The Will Of God

▶ How To Release The Powerful Forces That Guarantees Blessing

▶ The Incredible Role Of Your Memory & The Imagination

▶ The Hidden Power Of Imagination & How To Use It Properly

▶ The Difference Between The Love Of God And His Blessings

▶ 3 Steps In Increasing Your Faith

▶ 2 Rewards That Come When You Use Your Faith In God

▶ 7 Powerful Keys Concerning Your Faith

Dreams and desires begin as photographs within our hearts and minds - things that we want to happen in our future. God plants these pictures as invisible seeds within us. God begins every miracle in your life with a seed-picture... the invisible idea that gives birth to a visible blessing. In this teaching, you will discover your desires and how to concentrate on watering and nurturing the growth of your Dream-Seeds until you attain your God-given goals.

Wisdom Is The Principal Thing

Book B-11 / $9

Six Audio Tapes TS-02 / $30

The Wisdom Center

THE WISDOM CENTER

ORDER TODAY!
www.thewisdomcenter.cc

1-888-WISDOM-1
(1-888-947-3661)

THE WISDOM CENTER • P.O. Box 99 • Denton, Texas 76202

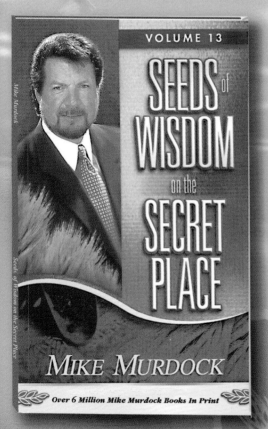

Run To Win.

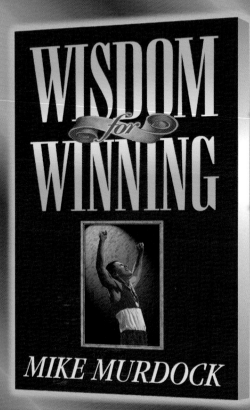

- ▸ **10 Ingredients For Success**
- ▸ **Ten Lies Many People Believe About Money**
- ▸ **20 Keys For Winning At Work**
- ▸ **20 Keys To A Better Marriage**
- ▸ **3 Facts Every Parent Should Remember**
- ▸ **5 Steps Out Of Depression**
- ▸ **The Greatest Wisdom Principle I Ever Learned**
- ▸ **7 Keys To Answered Prayer**
- ▸ **God's Master Golden Key To Total Success**
- ▸ **The Key To Understanding Life**

Everyone needs to feel they have achieved something with their life. When we stop producing, lonellness and laziness will choke all enthusiasm from our living. What would you like to be doing? What are you doing about it? Get started on a project in your life. Start building on your dreams. Resist those who would control and change your personal goals. Get going with this powerful teaching and reach your life goals!

ORDER TODAY!
www.thewisdomcenter.cc

1-888-WISDOM-1
(1-888-947-3661)

THE WISDOM CENTER • P.O. Box 99 • Denton, Texas 76202

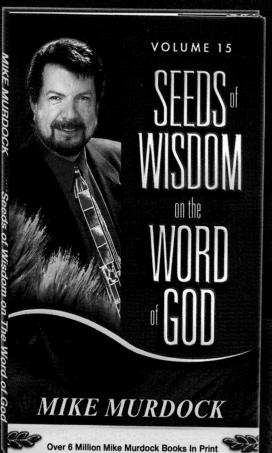

WISDOM COLLECTION

8

SECRETS OF THE UNCOMMON MILLIONAIRE

1. The Uncommon Millionaire Conference Vol. 1 (Six Cassettes)
2. The Uncommon Millionaire Conference Vol. 2 (Six Cassettes)
3. The Uncommon Millionaire Conference Vol. 3 (Six Cassettes)
4. The Uncommon Millionaire Conference Vol. 4 (Six Cassettes)
5. 31 Reasons People Do Not Receive Their Financial Harvest (256 Page Book)
6. Secrets of the Richest Man Who Ever Lived (178 Page Book)
7. 12 Seeds of Wisdom Books On 12 Topics
8. The Gift of Wisdom for Leaders Desk Calendar
9. Songs From The Secret Place (Music Cassette)
10. In Honor of the Holy Spirit (Music Cassette)
11. 365 Memorization Scriptures On The Word Of God (Audio Cassette)

Wisdom Is The Principal Thing

THE WISDOM COLLECTION 8
SECRETS OF THE UNCOMMON MILLIONAIRE

WC-08 /$195

The Wisdom Center

ORDER TODAY!
www.thewisdomcenter.cc

1-888-WISDOM-1
(1-888-947-3661)

THE WISDOM CENTER • P.O. Box 99 • Denton, Texas 76202